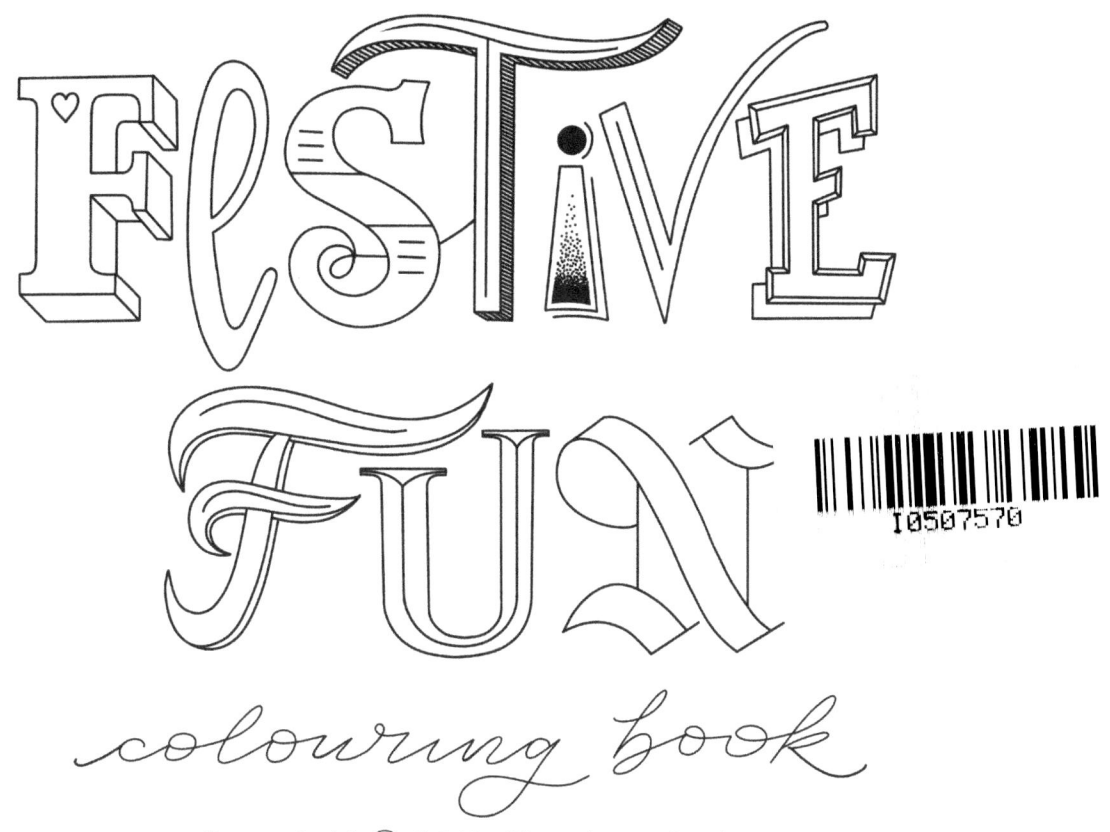

Copyright© 2018 Timeless Roots
All rights reserved.

No part of this publication may be reproduced,
stored in a retrieval system or transmitted in any
form or by any means, electronic, or mechanical, including
photocopy, recording or otherwise without the prior
permission in writing from the author Shivani Sharma.

www.timelessroots.co.uk

Share your creations with me on Instagram @timeless.roots

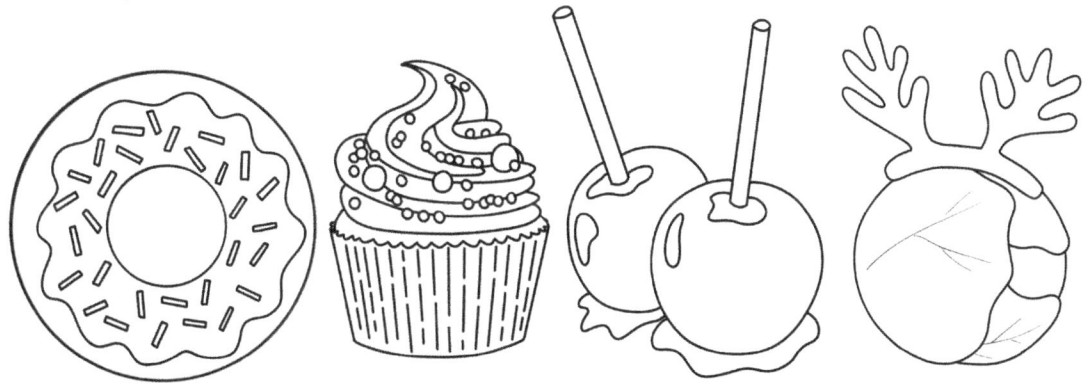

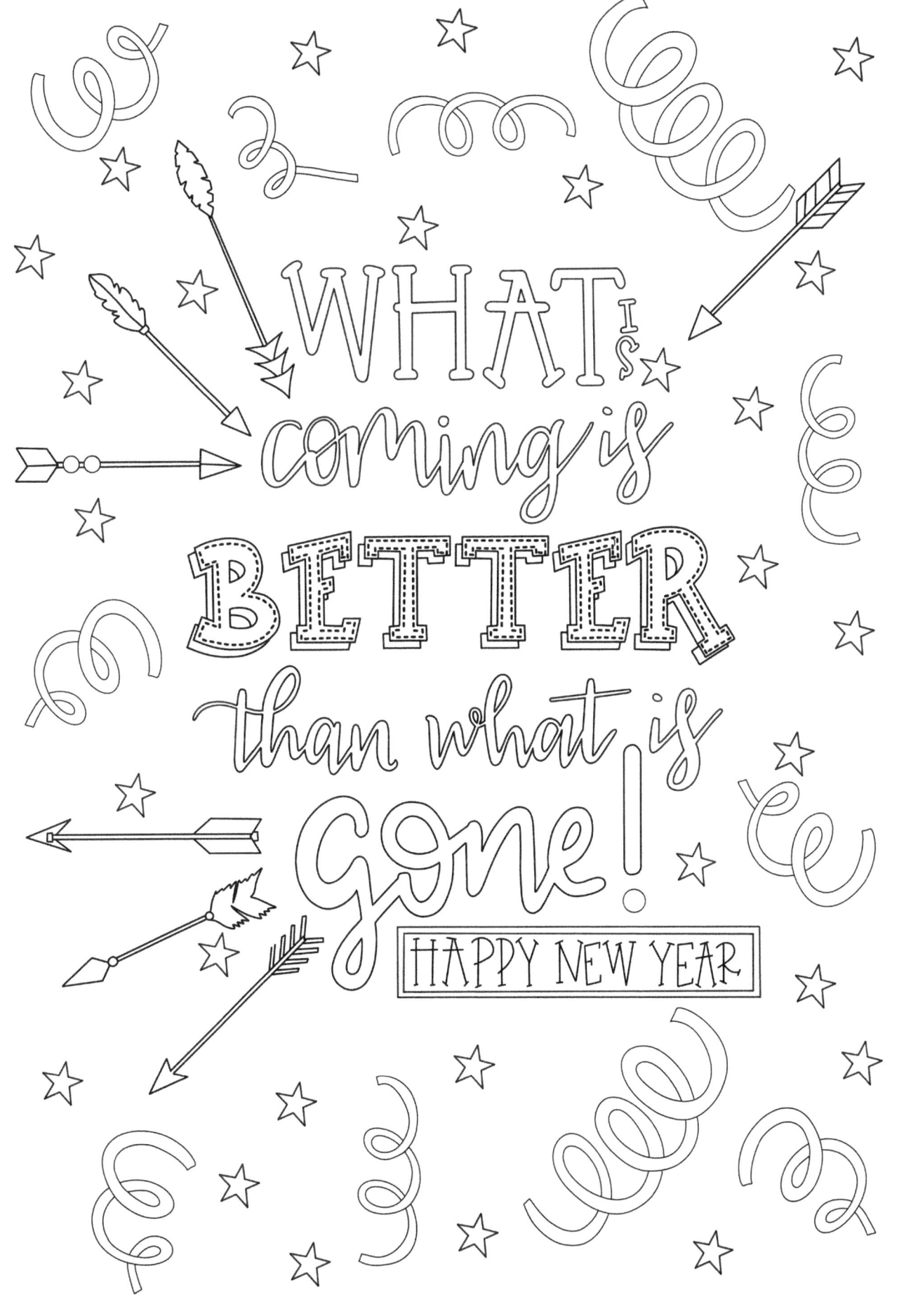

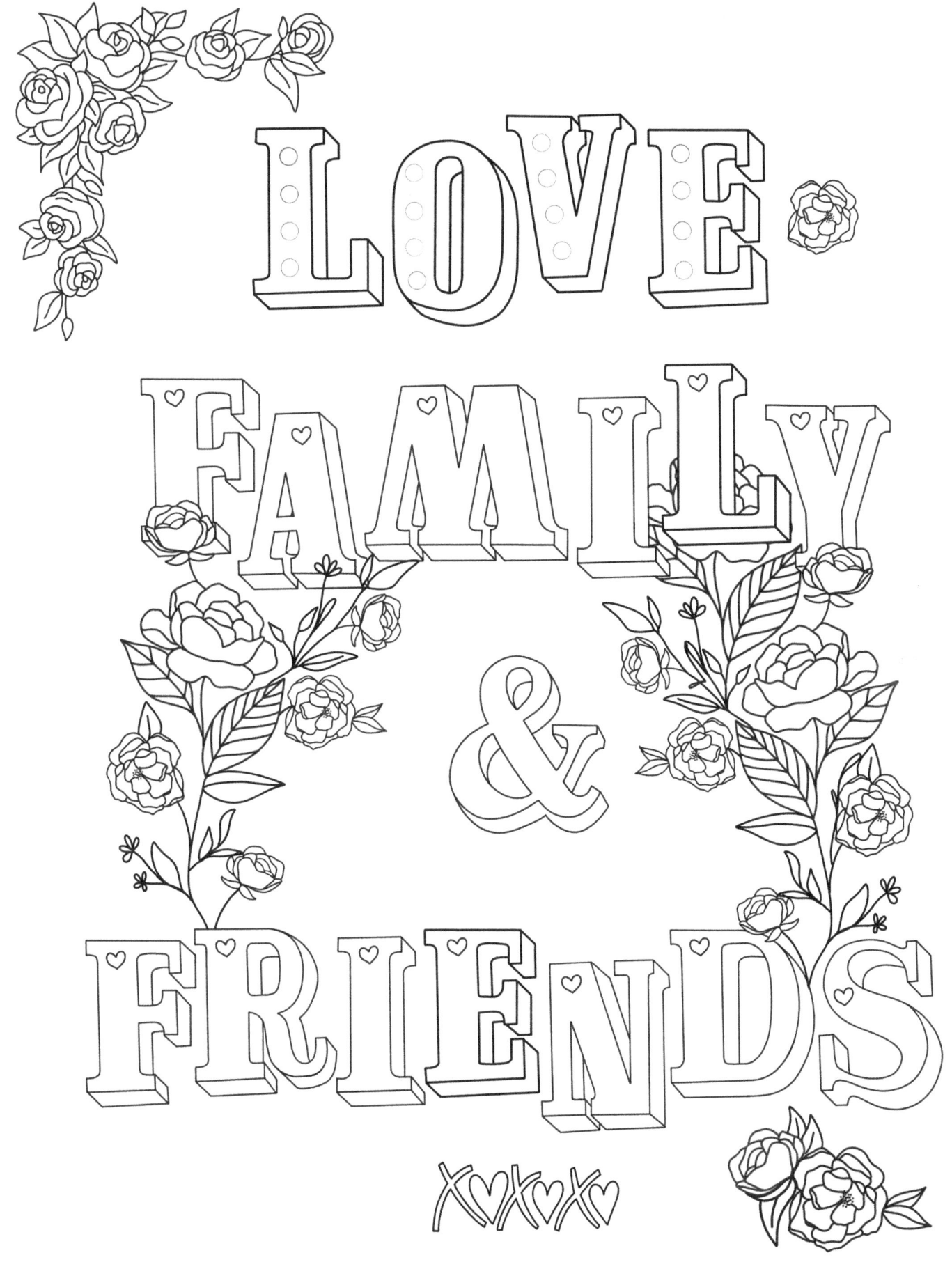

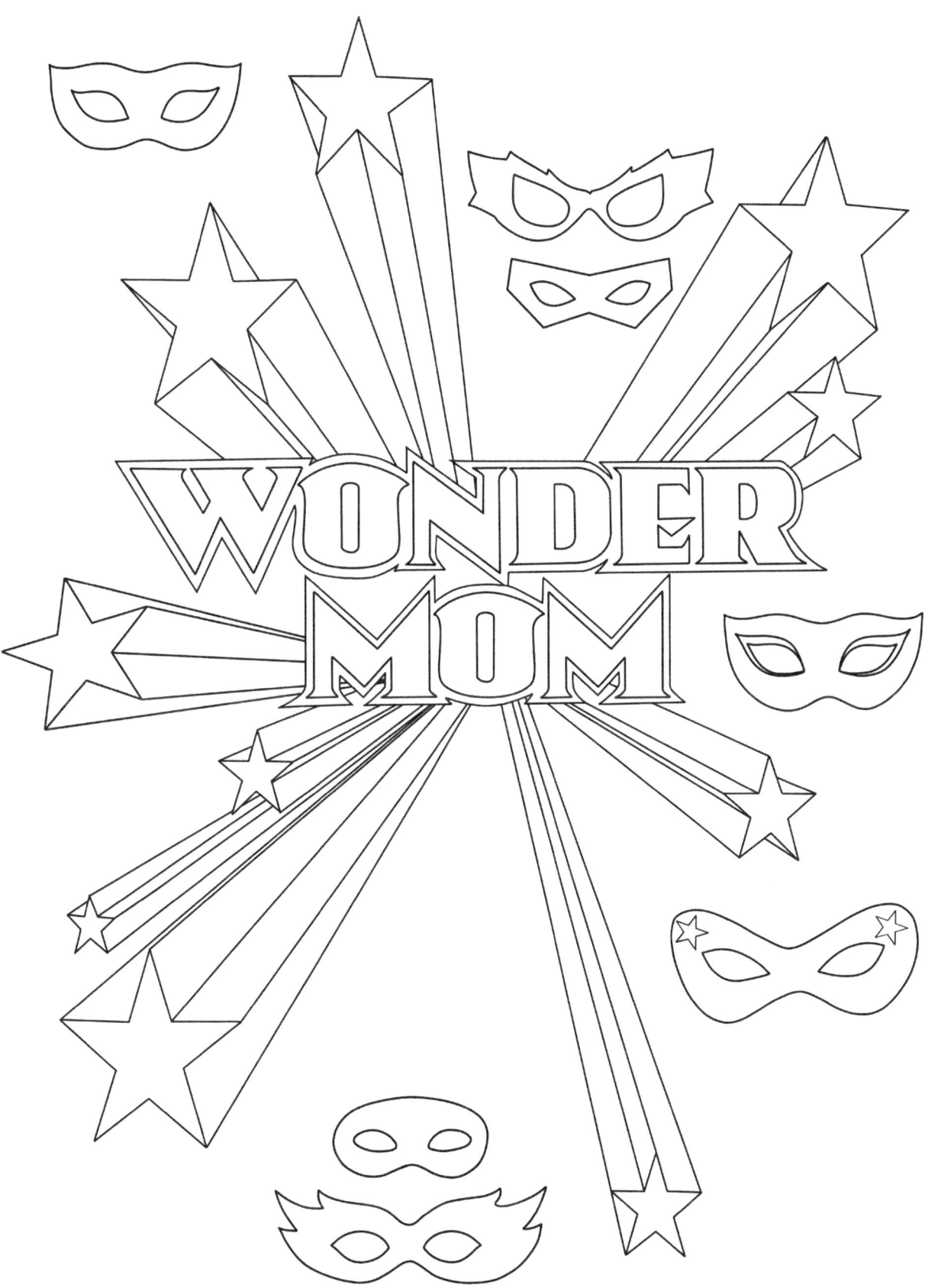

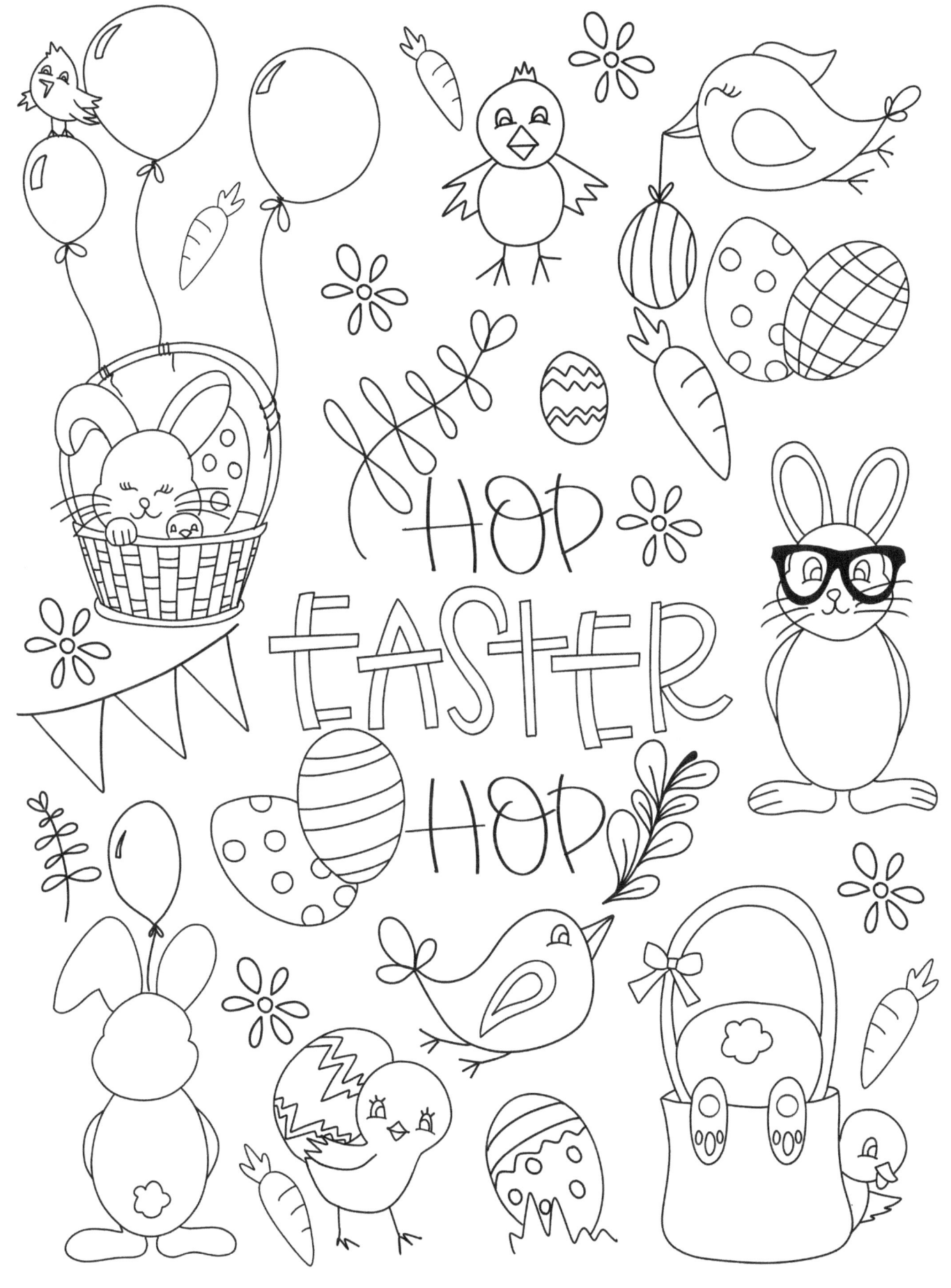

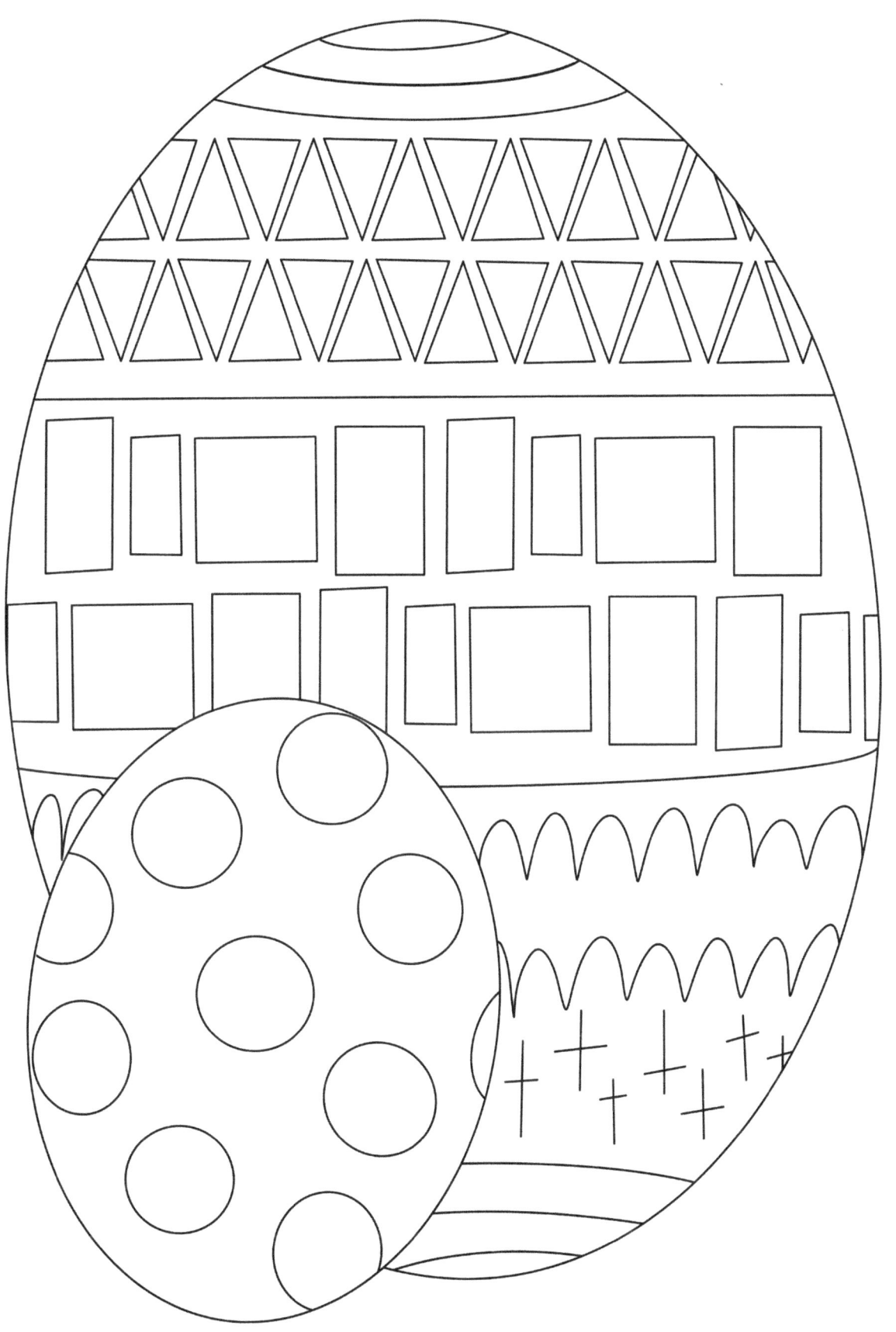

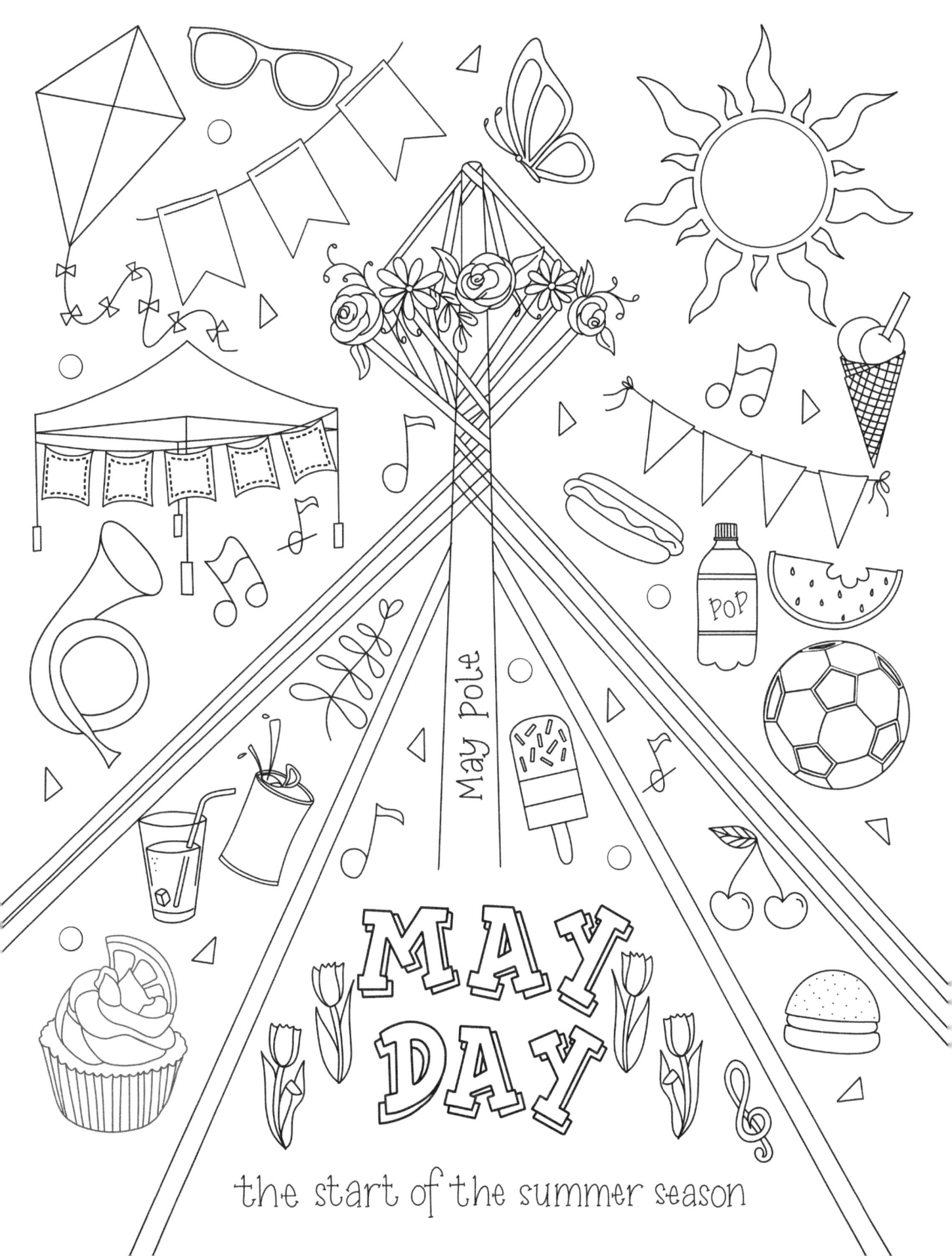

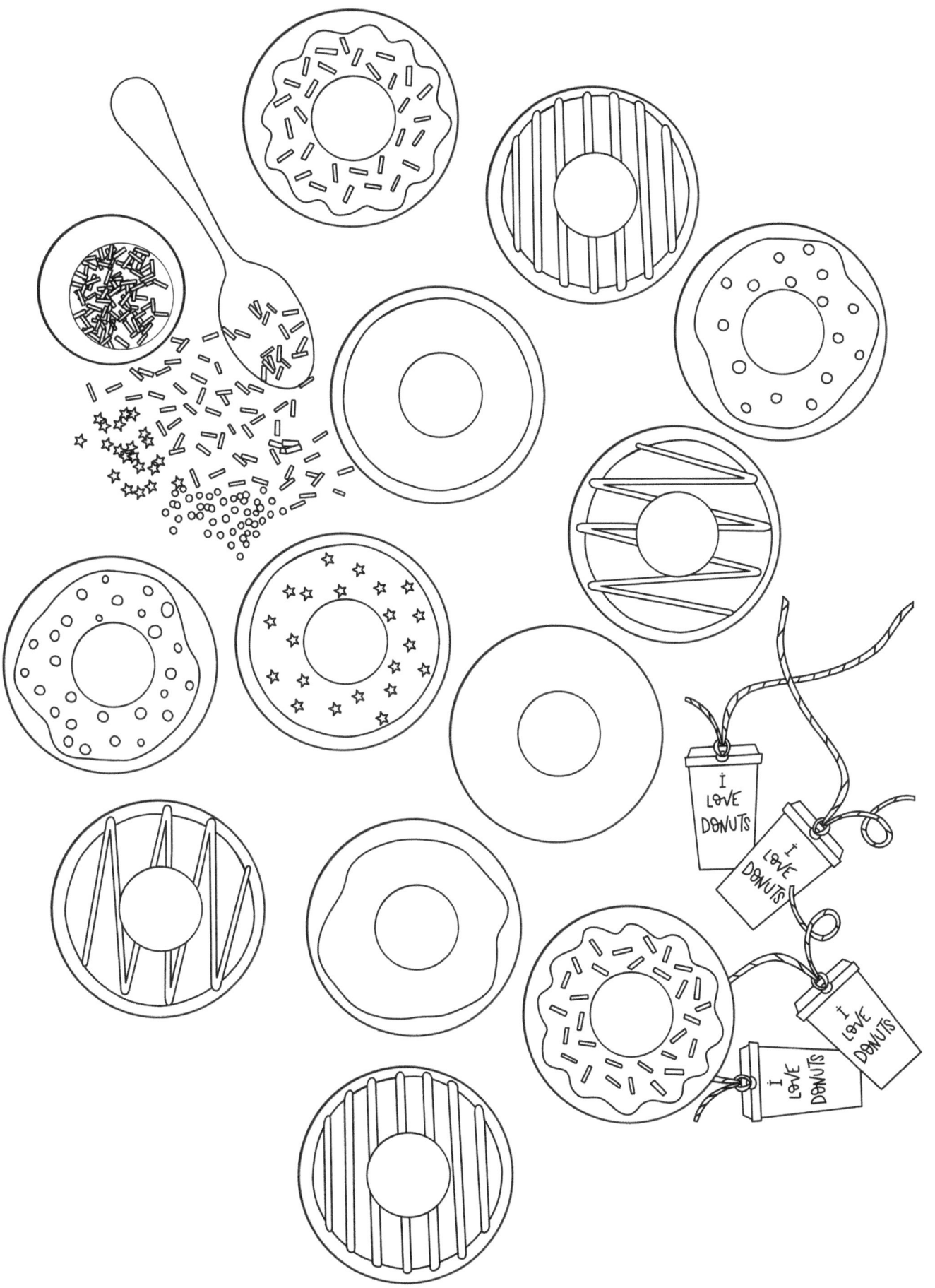

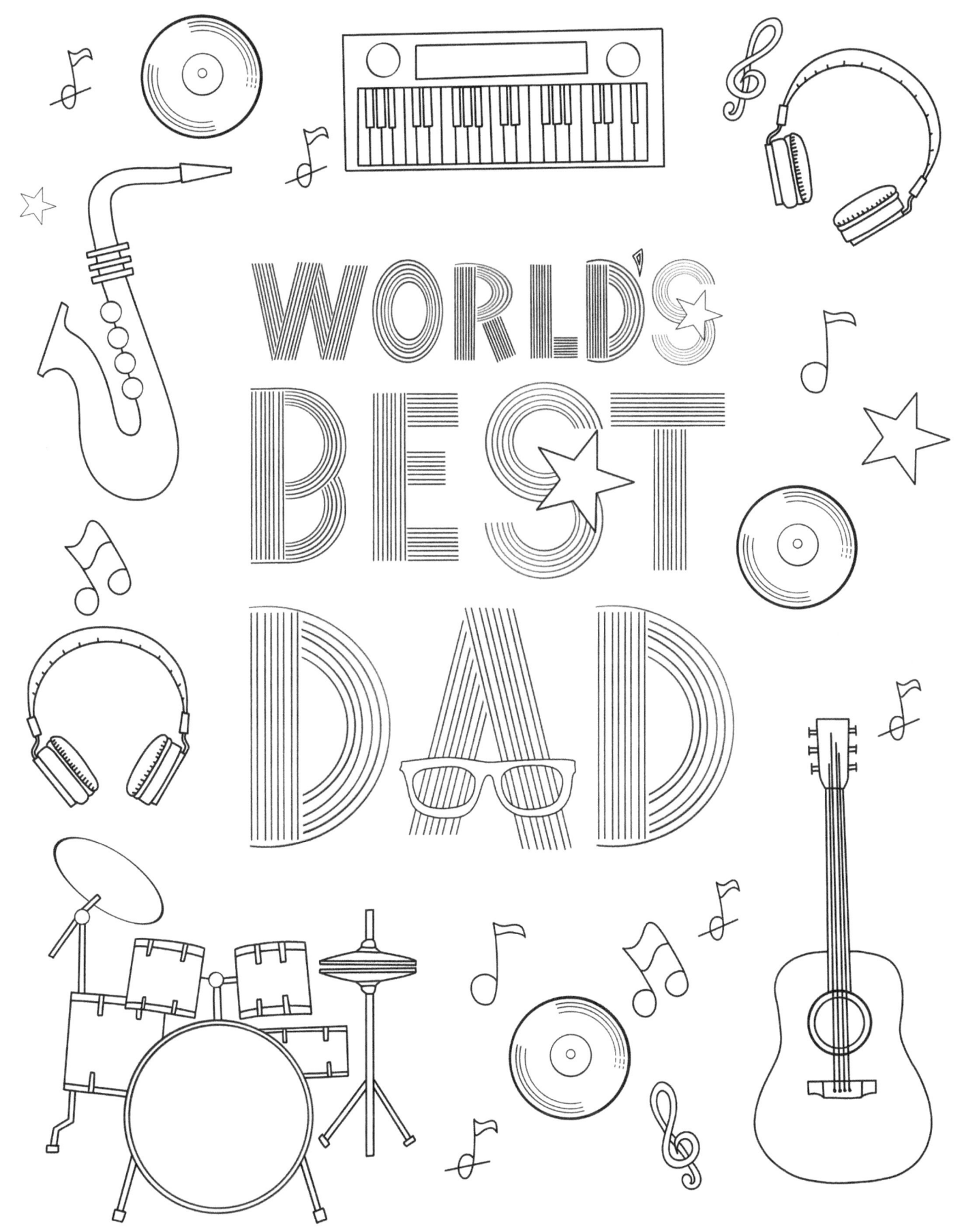

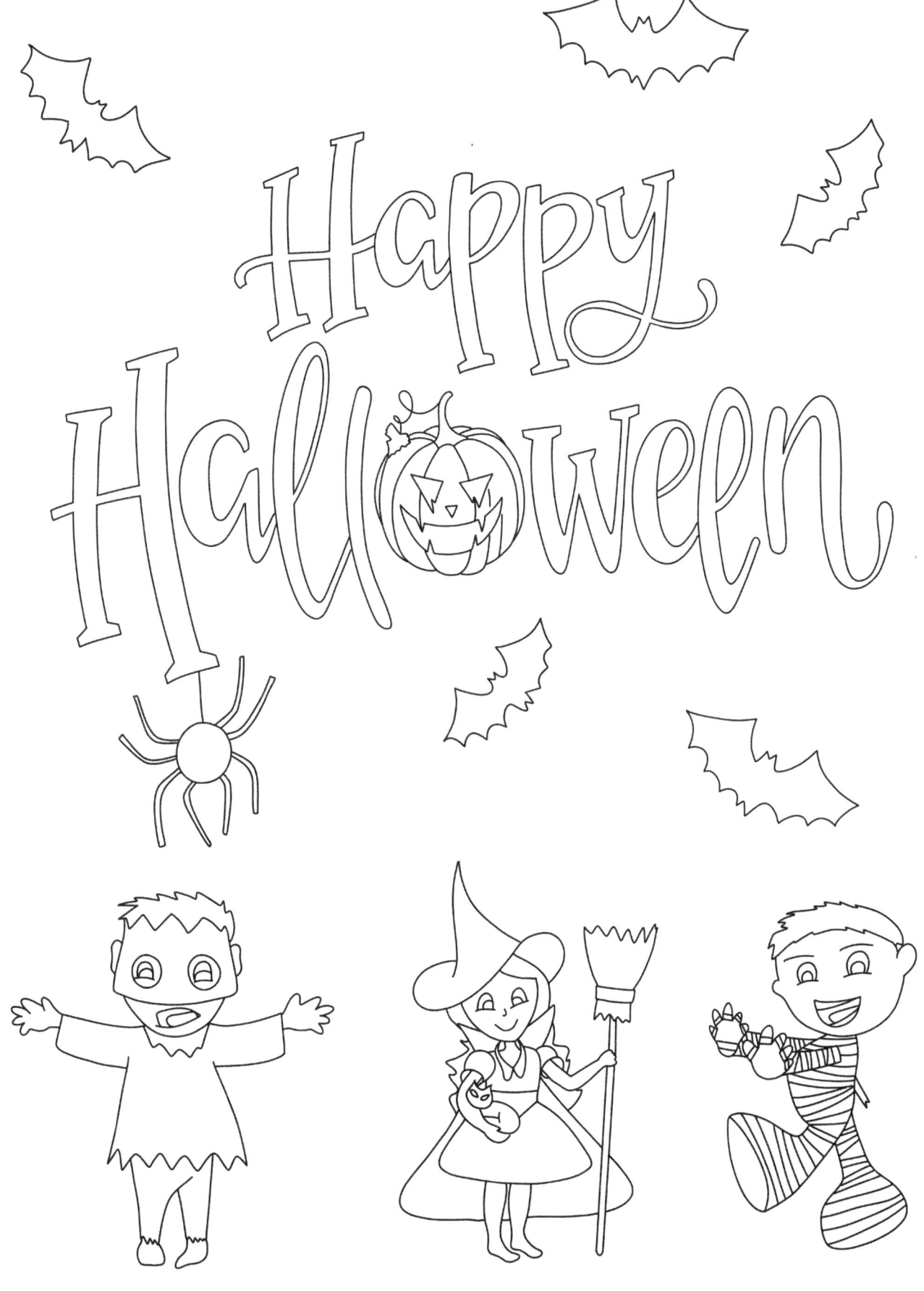

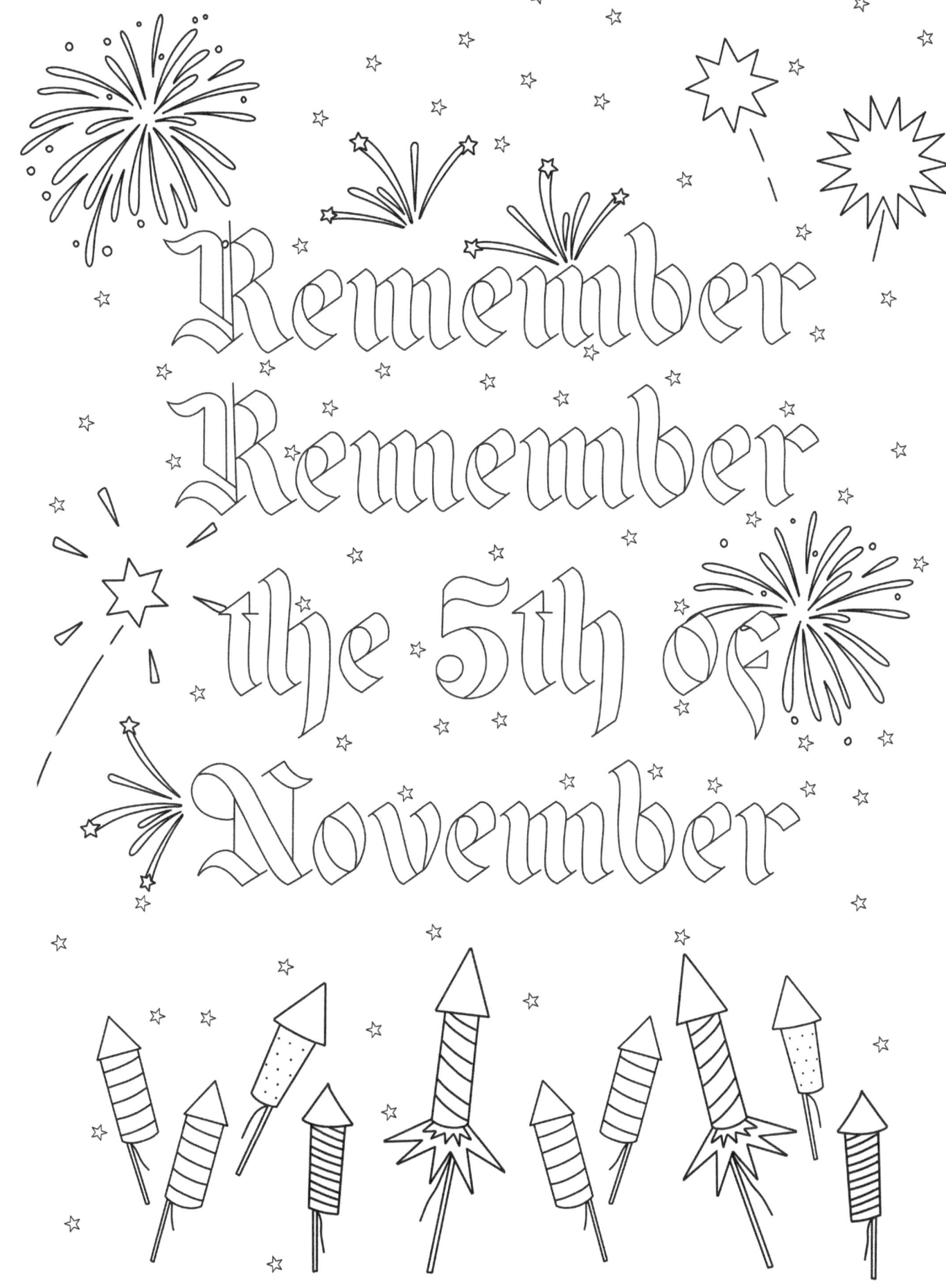

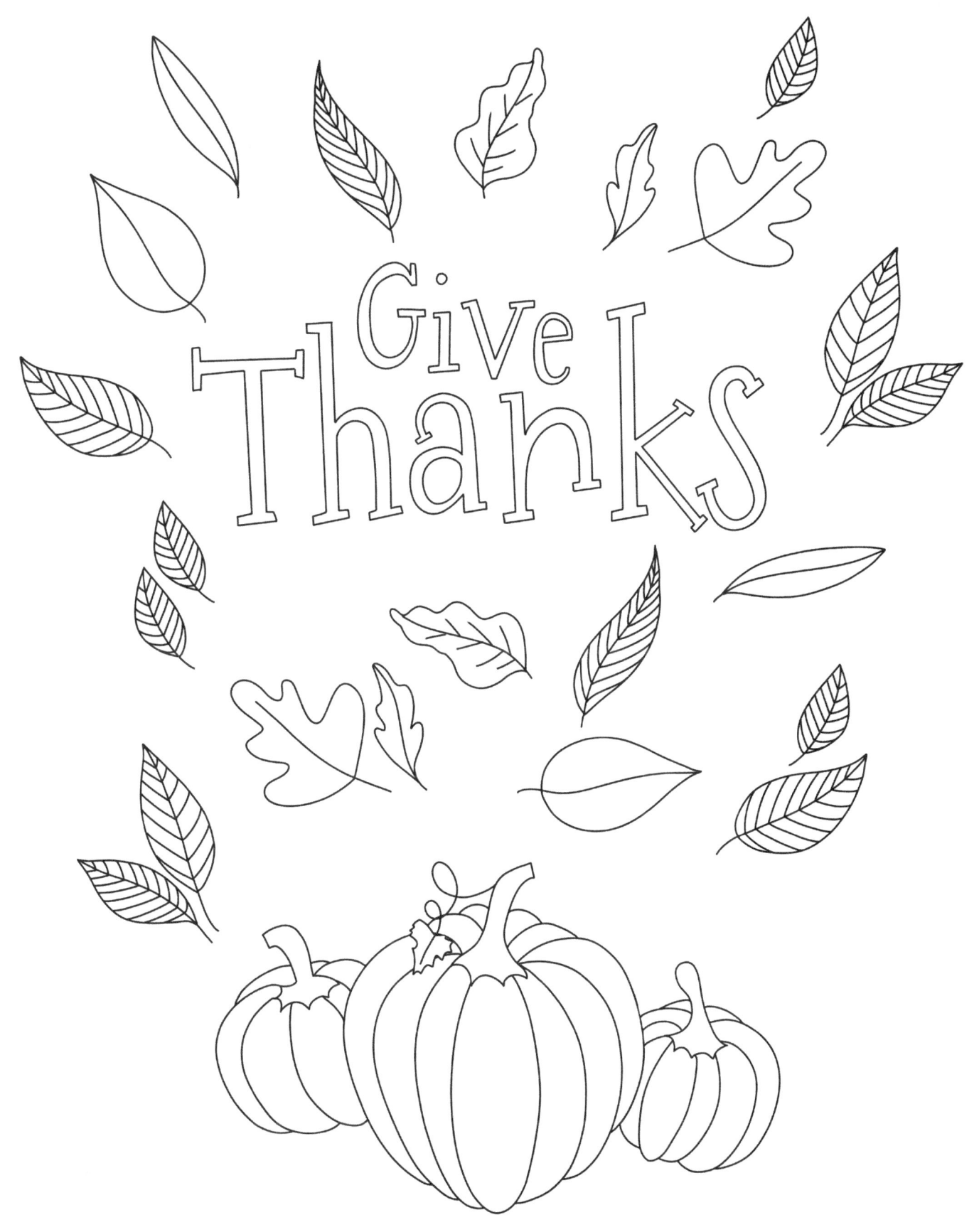

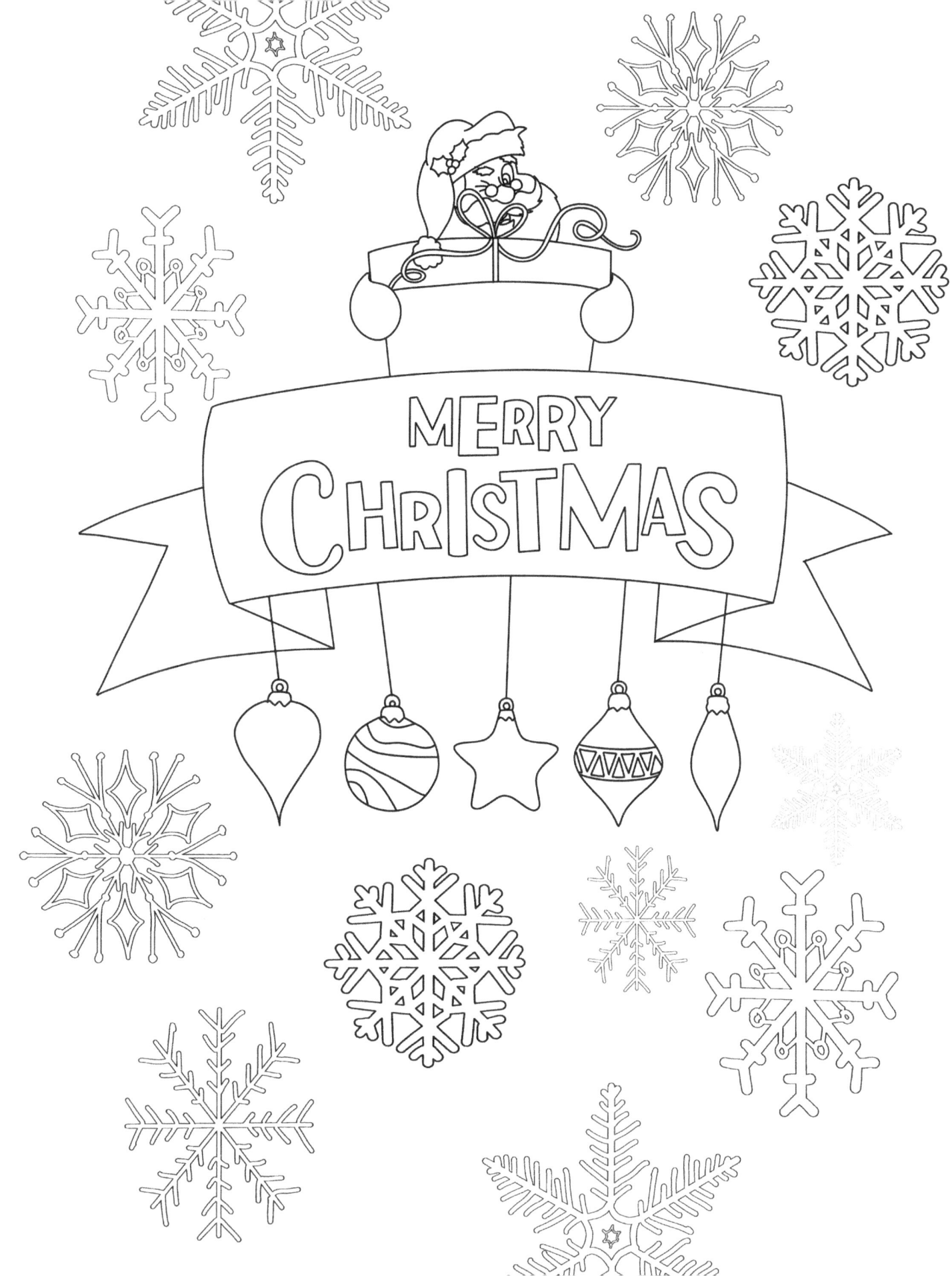

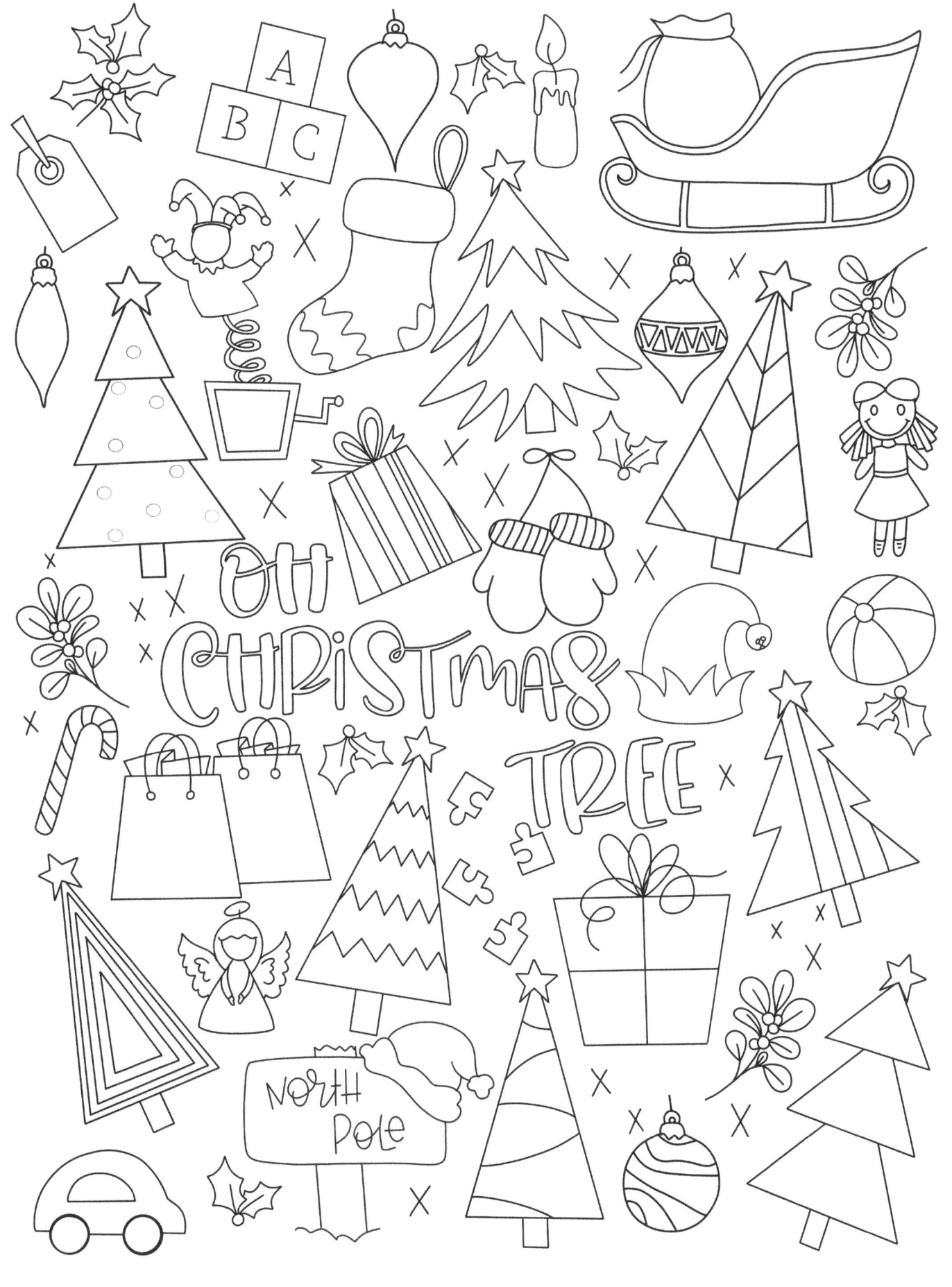

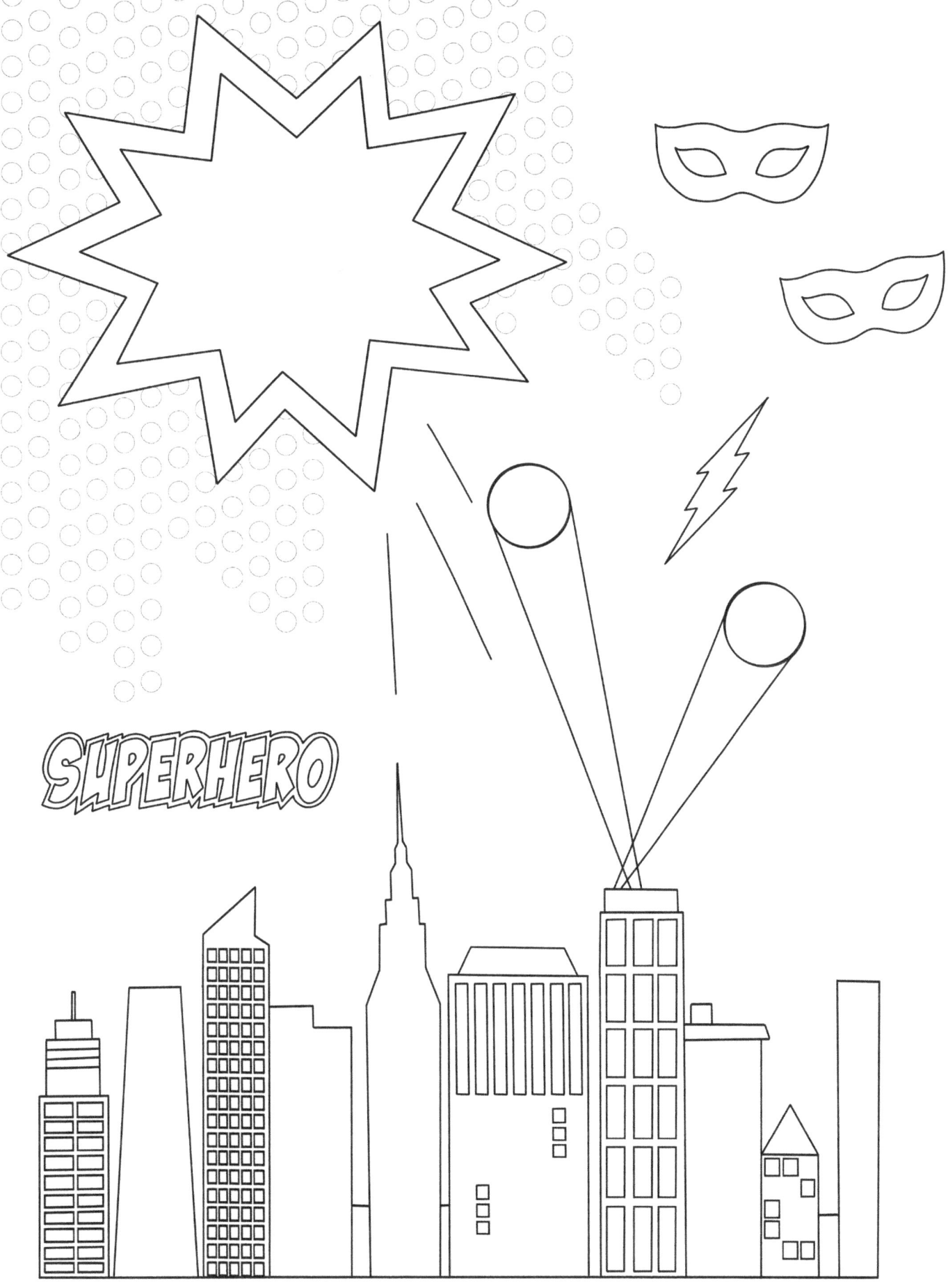

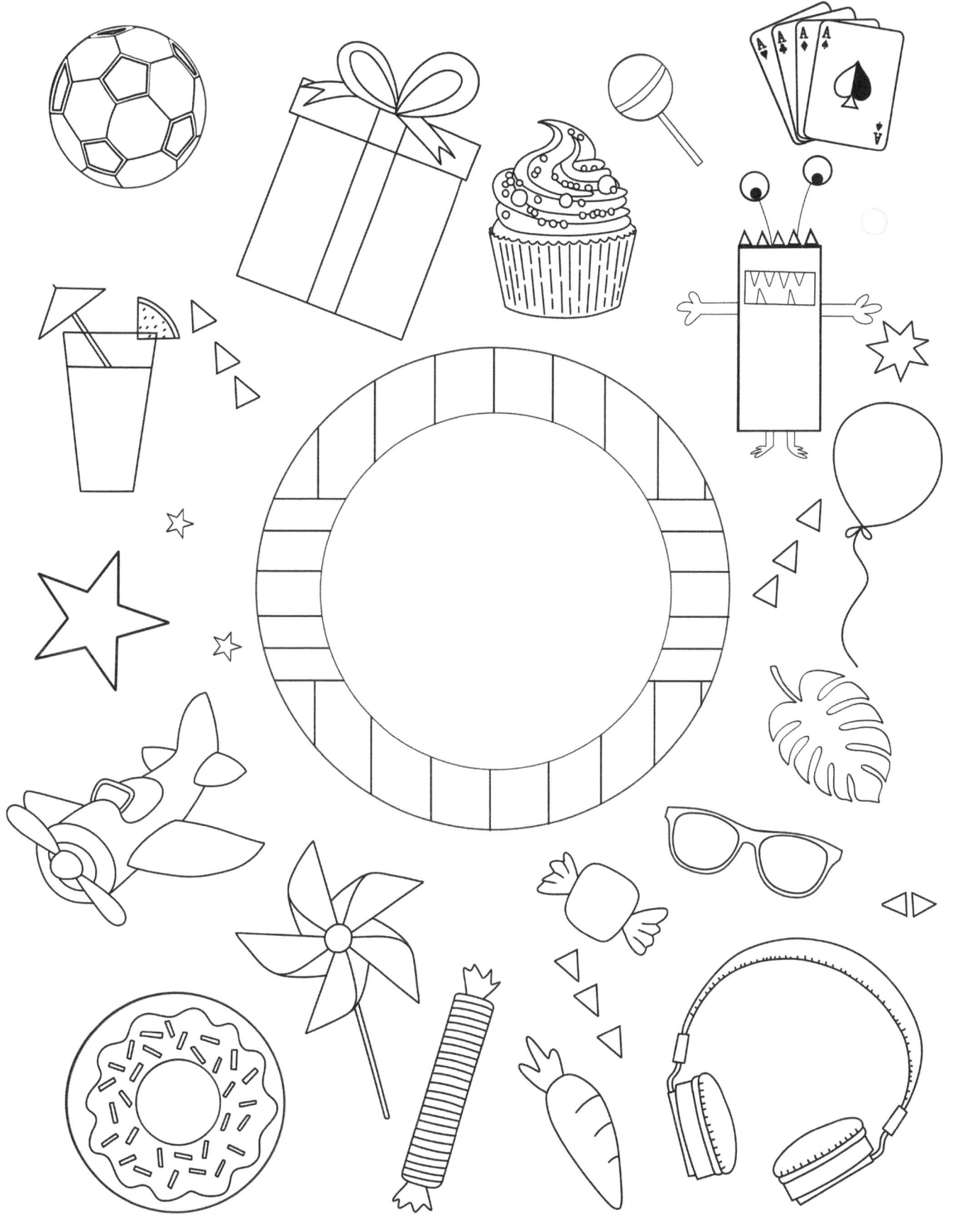

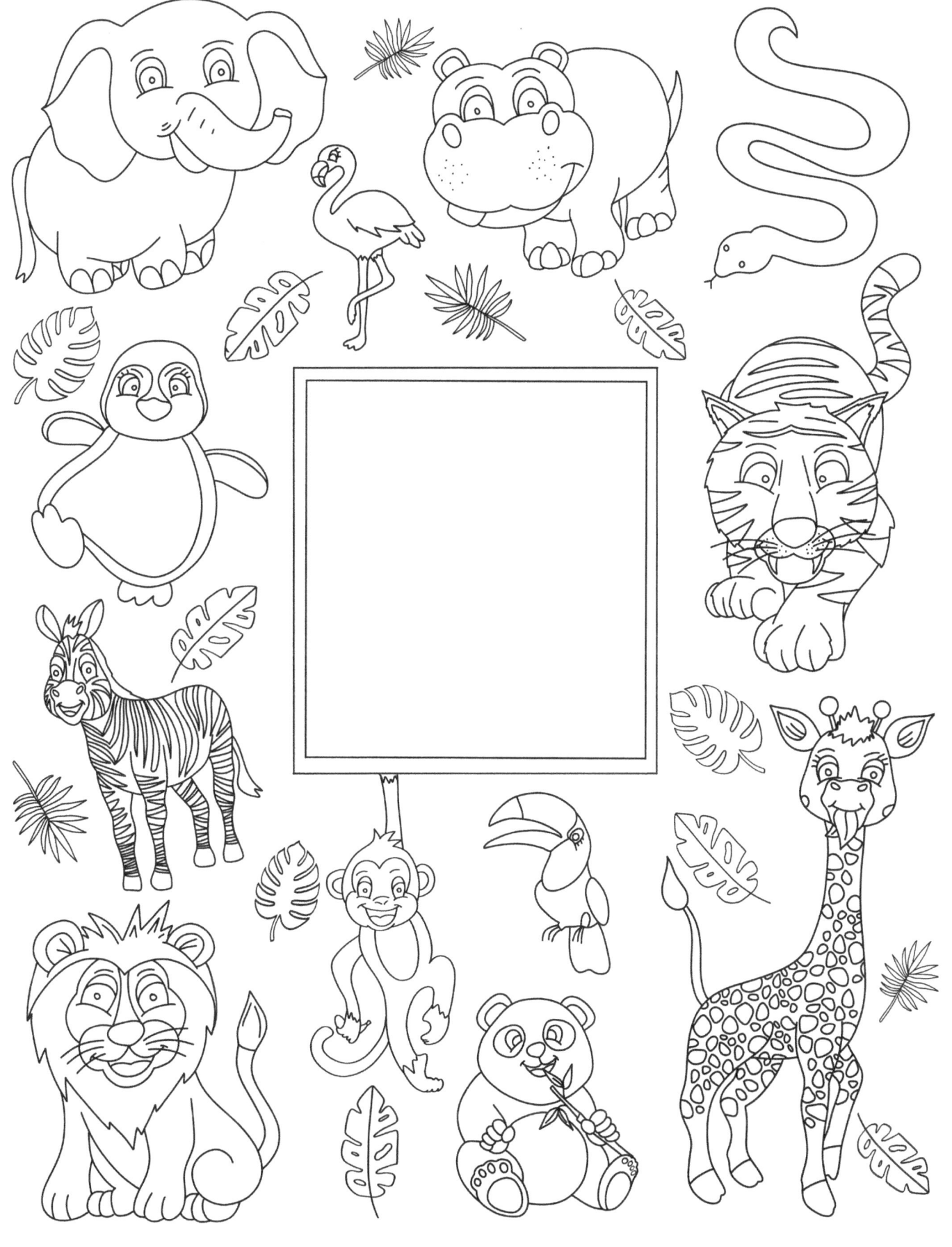

www.ingramcontent.com/pod-product-compliance
Lightning Source LLC
Chambersburg PA
CBHW082256220526
45469CB00009B/3031